Contents

Whiskered Wonders 1
Royal Bengal Tiger 6
Asiatic Lion 10
Leopard 14
Snow Leopard 18
Clouded Leopard 22
Fishing Cat 26
Caracal 30
Pallas's Cat 34
Eurasian Lynx 38
Desert Cat 42
Spot Them Here! 46
Fact Finder and Credits 47

Whiskered Wonders

India has the highest number of wild cat species in the world – 15! Wild cats occupy an important place in Indian culture. Whether it is in the national emblem (the Asiatic lion) or as the national animal (the Bengal tiger), the wild cats of India have commanded our respect for centuries. These remarkably adaptable felines are found across the country – from the snowy mountains of the Himalayas to the dense jungles of southern India, from the scorching Thar Desert to the unexplored caves of Northeast India.

Why Are Wild Cats Important?

Wild cats are the top predators in the food chain. They keep herbivore populations in check. Did you know that the mere presence of a wild cat prevents herbivores from staying in a place for too long and eating up all the plants? If wild cats are absent from an area, animals like deer, cattle and even small rodents like mice can overgraze and slow the growth of a forest or a grassland. Wild cats are the class monitors who maintain order in their habitats.

The high reaches of the Himalayas are home to the snow leopard

How Do Wild Cats Hunt?

All felines are carnivores. Wild cats have powerful jaws that crush bones, sharp claws that tear apart flesh and powerful limbs that help catch prey. All wild cats are ambush predators but their tactics may differ – tigers and leopards patiently wait to ambush their prey, while others like lions and caracals stalk their prey over long distances. Most are nocturnal hunters, which means they hunt at night, using their superb eyesight.

The Royal Bengal tiger, India's national animal

Do Wild Cats Live in Groups or Alone?

Lions are the only wild cats in India which live together in groups. All others are generally solitary, coming together only during breeding season. Some wild cats may babysit their siblings and relatives, but this is rare. These solitary animals fiercely defend their territories to protect food sources and mates. Wild cats mark their territories by spraying certain trees or rocks with their urine, scratching on tree bark with their sharp claws or emitting growls and roars.

How Are Wild Cats Different From Pet Cats?

Domestic cats have been around humans for at least 12,000 years and are used to human touch and presence. Despite many wild cats looking like domestic cats, they do not like to be around humans and find us a threat! Wild cats require large territories to hunt, breed and feel safe. Keeping wild cats as pets is a cruel practice that makes them unhappy and aggressive.

The Asiatic lion, found only in Gujarat, India

Royal Bengal Tiger

Find Me Here!

Popular places to spot them are Ranthambore National Park and Jim Corbett National Park.

CRITTER STATS

Scientific name: *Panthera tigris*
Size: 255–311 cm – bigger than a Royal Enfield bike!
Weight: 135–225 kg
Lifespan: 14–20 years
Habitat: forests, grasslands, mangrove swamps
Conservation status: endangered

The Royal Bengal tiger, India's national animal, is the largest and most iconic wild cat in India. The tiger is so important to the health of India's wildlife and forests that we created special areas to protect them, called tiger reserves.

The largest of India's wild cats, tigers evolved to be so big because of their preference for large prey such as sambar deer and gaur! If large prey are not available, they may even eat fish or smaller animals such as goats.

Like your fingerprints, each tiger's stripes are unique. They also act as camouflage. In forests and grasslands, the stripes blend in with shadows and sunlight. And since deer are colour-blind to orange, the tiger is almost invisible to them!

Not all hunts are successful. But when the tiger does succeed, escape is near-impossible. After stalking its prey, the cat will pounce in one powerful strike, enough to break the prey's spine.

Bengal tigers don't come in only orange and black! There are also white tigers, golden tigers and black tigers or pseudo-melanistic tigers.

These rare colours occur because of changes in genes, which are the building blocks of life present in the body's cells.

DID YOU KNOW?

Killing machines: Bengal tigers have the largest canines in the cat family at 3 inches long! This allows them to efficiently kill by chomping down on the prey's throat.

The Bengal tiger is found in India, Nepal, Bangladesh, Bhutan and south-western China. India has the largest population of Bengal tigers at around 3,600!

Roaring success: a tiger's roar can be heard over 3 km away! Tigers usually roar to warn other tigers against entering their territory.

Asiatic Lion

Find Me Here!

Found only in Gujarat, mainly in the Gir National Park but also in Pania, Mitiyala and Girnar sanctuaries.

CRITTER STATS

Scientific name: *Panthera leo*
Size: 160–250 cm – almost as long as a Maruti Alto
Weight: 110–190 kg
Lifespan: 16–21 years
Habitat: savannah grasslands and dry, open forests
Conservation status: endangered

India is the only place outside Africa where lions still live in the wild! The Asiatic lion is found only in India – and it's also the only wild cat here that lives in a group, called a pride. These lions are a proud part of India's history and culture. You can spot them on our national emblem, majestically facing all four directions.

Only male lions have manes – and the Asiatic lion's mane is smaller than the African lion's. That's how you can tell them apart!

The Asiatic lion's mane doesn't cover its ears or the top of its head. Instead, it looks more like a thick beard around its cheeks and chin.

A pride of Asiatic lions is dominated by females and could have up to 12 female lions living and hunting together while also taking care of each others' cubs. Males may form small groups of up to 3 and visit the pride to eat, mate or spend time with their cubs.

Like any other big cat, lions need an abundance of large prey to feed their prides. An adult lion needs 2,500-3,600 kg of meat per year to be healthy! Favourite dinner menu items include chital, sambar deer, nilgai and water buffalo.

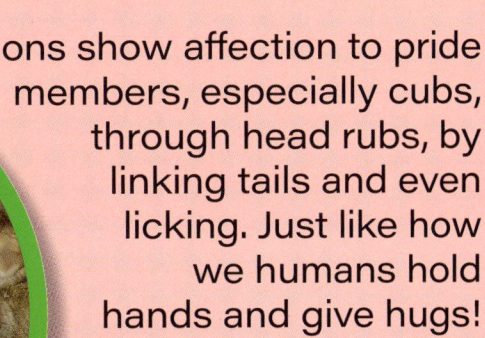

Lions show affection to pride members, especially cubs, through head rubs, by linking tails and even licking. Just like how we humans hold hands and give hugs!

 DID YOU KNOW?

More than one-fourth of India's lion population lives outside the wildlife sanctuaries created for it. Many of them even live alongside humans. Imagine waking up to a lion on your doorstep one morning!

Girl power: lionesses do most of the hunting. Male lions rarely hunt. They usually join the pride just in time for dinner and often eat first, taking the lion's share of the meat.

Leopard

Find Me Here!
Everywhere in India, except for the desert areas of Gujarat and Rajasthan and the upper Himalayas.

CRITTER STATS

Scientific name: *Panthera pardus*
Size: 180–240 cm (with tail) – like a single bed!
Weight: 30–75 kg
Lifespan: 12–17 years
Habitat: jungles, fields and even near our homes
Conservation status: near threatened

Leopards are the only wild cats found across India – not only in jungles and savannahs, but also on the edges of towns and agricultural fields. Despite being so widespread, their shy, secretive nature makes them hard to study.

A leopard's golden-brown, flower-shaped spots are called rosettes. They are usually larger on the body and hind legs of the leopard. Rosettes help them blend into vegetation. Like a tiger's stripes, a leopard's rosettes are unique to each leopard.

Remember Bagheera, Mowgli's friend from *The Jungle Book*? He was a black or melanistic leopard. Black leopards are also called panthers. But they are not entirely black! If you look closely, you can see the rosettes against their fur.

Leopards are often confused with cheetahs. But they are two separate species that are also different to look at. For example, leopard spots are flower-shaped, while cheetahs have plain, round spots. If you spot a "cheetah" in India, it is most probably a leopard!

Leopards are the most athletic of the big cats. They can swim, run at up to 50–60 km/h, leap 6.5 m in front and 3.5 m upwards, are excellent tree climbers and can carry up to 20 kg of prey up a tree! Leopards often hide their kill in trees, away from tigers who may want to steal it.

Despite being found all over India, leopards face a lot of threats to their existence. They are hunted by poachers for their beautiful fur, sharp teeth and claws. Leopards also lose out when their habitats are destroyed for construction or to make new crop fields.

 # DID YOU KNOW?

Leopards can go up to 10 days without drinking water. Instead, they get their moisture from the blood of their prey. This allows them to survive life in arid zones and dry grasslands!

These cats have black-and-white spots on the backs of their ears resembling little eyes! These "false eyes" may scare off predators by making them think the leopard is watching from behind.

Leopard calls sound like someone is sawing wood using a handsaw!

Snow Leopard

Find Me Here!
2,000–6,000m high rocky, snow-clad mountains of Ladakh, Uttarakhand and Arunachal Pradesh.

CRITTER STATS

Scientific name: *Panthera uncia*
Size: 1–1.3m – like a large German shepherd
Lifespan: 15–18 years in the wild
Habitat: above the Himalayan treeline and the Trans-Himalayas
Conservation status: vulnerable

The Himalayas whisper of a ghost that lives in the highest peaks, jumps down the steepest cliffs without injury and is said to be the guardian of the mountains. No, this is not an actual ghost but the elusive snow leopard.

Snow leopards are the largest predators of the frozen peaks and icy deserts that make up the high Himalayas and Trans-Himalayas, a cold desert region beyond the mountains. It hunts down animals such as the bharal and yak.

Massive furry paws help it run through snow, and strong, short front limbs and longer hind limbs help it jump up to 30 feet (10 m) in one leap!

The snow leopard has dense, 12-cm-long fur and short, round ears to keep warm. Its thick fatty tail is used as a blanket, and the short wide nose heats the air before it reaches the lungs.

These cats are called the ghost of the Himalayas for a reason! Their grey-white fur and dark rosettes help them blend perfectly into the surroundings. Their camouflage is so good that the animal is almost invisible!

 # DID YOU KNOW?

Although called leopards, snow leopards are genetically closer to tigers than leopards.

Snow leopards are not only found in India. They are also found in Pakistan, China, Afghanistan and central Asian countries.

Snow leopards have the longest tail among all cat species. They use their thick, furry, muscular tail like a blanket on cold nights and for balance on steep cliffs!

Clouded Leopard

Find Me Here!
Found in the tropical evergreen and deciduous forests of Northeast India.

CRITTER STATS

Scientific name: *Neofelis nebulosa*
Size: 130–200 cm – about the size of a street dog
Weight: 11–23 kg
Lifespan: up to 13 years in the wild, 11–17 years in captivity
Habitat: hills and lower Himalayas of Northeast India
Conservation status: vulnerable

When you think of animals that can hang down from trees, you usually imagine a monkey. But did you know there is a wild cat that can do this too? Meet the clouded leopard – the most mysterious of India's "big cats".

Clouded leopards have some of the most beautiful pelts (the fur and skin of an animal) in the cat world. The coat colour ranges from hues of brown to grey, with large, dusky-grey blotched patterns resembling clouds.

Their tails are as long as their bodies. This extra-long tail allows them to maintain balance when climbing trees.

Very few cats can climb down a tree head first or upside down, or even hang from a branch by their hind legs. But a clouded leopard can do all this with ankles that can rotate 180 degrees to allow for these arboreal (which means up on a tree) gymnastics.

Sometimes, if they are on a tree and spot a squirrel or a mouse deer passing by, they may hang from the tree's branch using their back feet and whoosh – snatch up their prey from the forest floor!

💡 DID YOU KNOW?

The clouded leopard was officially recorded as a species only 200 years ago. But they are so mysterious, we know just as little about them now as we did 200 years ago! It is Meghalaya's state animal.

The clouded leopard's species name *"Nebulosa"* comes from the Latin word *nebula* which means clouds – referring to the hazy, cloud-like spots on its coat.

Fishing Cat

Find Me Here!
In large wetlands, near rivers and swamps like Chilika Lake in Odisha and the Sundarbans.

CRITTER STATS
Scientific name: *Prionailurus viverrinus*
Size: 78–108 cm – about twice the size of a house cat
Weight: 5–17 kg
Lifespan: 10–12 years
Habitat: wetlands, marshes and mangroves
Conservation status: vulnerable

What barks like a dog but is not a dog? A fishing cat, that's what! Meet this unique small cat which is a pro-swimmer, goes fishing and has webbed feet. Living true to the stereotype of cats loving fish, the fishing cat spends its days in and around water bodies, diving for fish, small crabs and snails.

Fishing cats will stand by a water's edge and gently tap the surface to lure fish in, mimicking the movement of insects on water. And the minute an unsuspecting fish swims close by, zap – the fishing cat swiftly snaps it up!

If sitting by the water proves unsuccessful for a catch, fishing cats may swim to catch fish or even ambush waterbirds from underwater! They have webbed feet like frogs and a short, flat and powerful tail to help them swim better.

Living in and around wetlands means fishing cats need to get used to being wet. They have a built-in diving suit in the form of glossy, yellowish-gray, double-layered fur with an inner, short-haired layer that is waterproof. This keeps them warm and dry underwater.

Being a small creature living among tall wetland grasses requires fishing cats to come up with innovative ways of finding each other. They communicate through a variety of interesting sounds such as barks, low growls, duck-like quacks and low-pitched meows.

 DID YOU KNOW?

Mama's pet: fishing cat kittens, like all feline kittens, learn to hunt by watching their mothers. They become independent at 10 months.

Claws out: fishing cats are the only small cats in India who keep their claws sticking out of their toes. This helps them grasp fish underwater. All other Indian small cats retract their claws when not in use to keep them sharp.

Caracal

Find Me Here!
Dry areas of Rajasthan, Gujarat and Madhya Pradesh.

CRITTER STATS

Family: *Caracal caracal*
Size: 61–106 cm – about the size of a small cycle
Weight: 8–20 kg
Lifespan: 10–12 years
Habitat: arid areas, scrub and rocky outcrops
Conservation status: least concern

Images in this chapter are of a caracal subspecies seen outside India. But in appearance, it is similar to the one seen in India.

The caracal, or *syah-gosh* in Persian, is probably India's rarest cat. This elusive predator has been part of India's history and culture for centuries, but is now largely forgotten because so few caracals remain in India.

Although widespread in other parts of the world, the caracal is critically endangered in India due to poaching and habitat loss. We have less than 120 caracals left! Spotting one in the wild is extremely rare.

Back when kings used to rule the land, caracals were trained to hunt game birds such as pigeons, francolins and bustards. Competitions used to be held to count how many pigeons a caracal could catch!

Caracals are built to survive and thrive in harsh desert environments. Its tawny, sand-coloured pelt offers great camouflage in dry and desert areas. Its paws are lined with long, stiff hair which helps it walk and run silently on loose desert sand.

When a caracal spots a bird, it ambushes it in the blink of an eye. Most cats would miss the bird as soon as it flies. But not the caracal. It uses its powerful hind legs to leap almost 10 feet (3 m) high, changing directions mid-air. One swipe of its powerful paws, and the bird is in the bag.

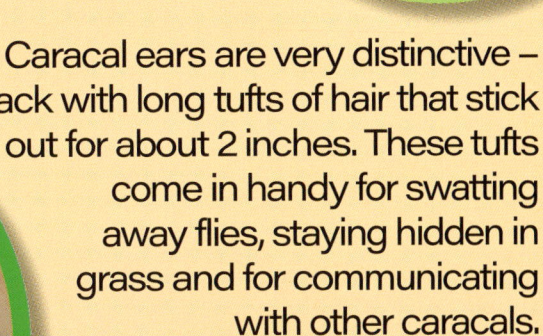

Caracal ears are very distinctive – black with long tufts of hair that stick out for about 2 inches. These tufts come in handy for swatting away flies, staying hidden in grass and for communicating with other caracals.

 DID YOU KNOW?

Caracal ears stand out. Did you know caracals have 20 muscles in their ears? This helps them detect even the quietest footsteps of a mouse in the desert!

Like most cats, caracals are nocturnal and hunt during the night. In India they mostly survive on rodents, unlike in other countries where they hunt larger mammals and big birds.

Have you ever seen a house cat "make biscuits" by kneading? Caracals do that too! Caracals have scent glands on their toes and when they knead a surface, they mark that area as their territory.

Pallas's Cat

Find Me Here!

Best seen at Changthang Wildlife Sanctuary in Ladakh and the Trans-Himalayan region of north Sikkim.

CRITTER STATS

Family: *Otocolobus manul*
Length: 45–65 cm – about the size of a pomeranian
Weight: 2.5–4.5 kg
Lifespan: 6–8 years in the wild
Habitat: rocky areas in the cold desert beyond the Himalayas
Conservation status: least concern

Have you seen a cat that always looks grumpy? That's the Pallas's cat, or manul, with its flat face, squinty eyes and fluffy cheeks! But it's not really angry – that's just its natural look. These secretive cats live in remote, rocky places in the Trans-Himalayas and blend in perfectly with their surroundings. Their amazing camouflage makes spotting a Pallas's cat a rare and lucky sight!

In India, Pallas's cats live in very cold, rocky, Himalayan deserts. These solitary cats choose abandoned marmot (a large mountain rodent) burrows and rocky caves for their homes. Litters of 2-6 kittens are housed in these warm and cosy dens, away from the snow and predators.

Pallas's cats have the longest and densest fur in the cat world. This keeps them warm in their freezing mountain habitats. They even stand on their thick, furry tails to avoid stepping on cold, wet snow.

Pallas's cats are known for periscope-like behaviour when in danger or during hunts. They hide behind rocks and bob their heads up and down – just like a submarine's periscope – to peek out and check for food or danger!

Pallas's cats' pupils contract to small circles to control how much light enters the eye. This possibly helps them calculate how far away a prey is.

DID YOU KNOW?

Their hunting success rate is only 30 per cent, but Pallas's cats are still important for keeping mountain rodent numbers in check.

Although Pallas's cats are big and fluffy looking, they are actually quite tiny underneath all that fur – no bigger than a normal house cat. Without the fur, they weigh less than a house cat.

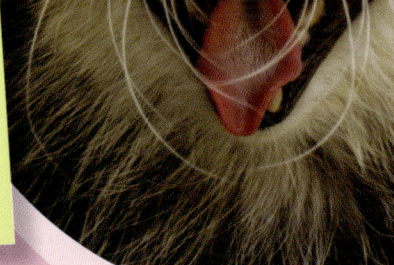

Eurasian Lynx

Find Me Here!

Ladakh, Sikkim and Jammu and Kashmir are the best places to spot this fascinating animal.

CRITTER STATS

Family: *Lynx lynx*
Length: 96–130 cm – about the size of a small bicycle
Weight: 12–32 kg
Lifespan: 10–15 years in the wild
Habitat: cold rocky deserts and rocky areas in the Himalayas
Conservation Status: near threatened

Quiet, mysterious and a creature celebrated in stories for its sharp eyesight and brains, the Eurasian lynx is one of the least studied of Himalayan wild cats. This medium-sized mountain dweller lives in the high, rocky deserts and scrublands of the Himalayas, hunting woolly hare, pika, mountain voles, Himalayan marmots and goats.

Eurasian lynxes have stocky bodies, powerful legs and large, furry snowshoe-like paws to help them travel long distances and hunt through thick snow and rocky terrain.

They can take leaps of several metres, climb steep rocky mountains and run at lightning speeds using their muscular legs – useful skills when hunting superfast animals such as hares and foxes.

Lynxes have sideburns, tufted ears and silvery beards. The tufted ears help them hear sounds accurately and act as a protection from harsh winds. The lynx's short tail helps reduce heat and energy loss.

To survive in a place where winds are freezing and harsh, food is scarce and animals are fast, you need to be able to spot prey as soon as it appears. Lynx eyes work overtime during both night and day, to help them spot dinner on the move.

 DID YOU KNOW?

Lynx mamas make carefully constructed nests for their kittens, under rocks or trees with drooping branches. They line their nests with feathers, deer hair and dry grass to make cosy beds for their babies.

Lynxes travel more than 20 km in a night to patrol and guard their territories, making sure competing lynxes don't enter their area.

Lynxes are known to be cannibals, a rarity among cats. 5 per cent to 8 per cent of their diet consists of other lynxes.

Desert Cat

Find Me Here!
Found in the Thar Desert and arid, thorny scrub forests of Rajasthan, Gujarat, Madhya Pradesh.

CRITTER STATS
Family: *Felis lybica ornata*
Length: 47–60 cm – like a large house cat
Weight: 2–4 kg
Lifespan: up to 11 years
Habitat: arid and semi-arid regions
Conservation status: vulnerable

Meet the Indian desert cat – wild, tiny and hard to spot! With its sandy coat and pointy ears, it looks almost like a house cat, but don't be fooled. This shy feline lives in hot, dry deserts and sneaks through the sand like a shadow. You might spot it crossing a sand dune, but it always stays just out of reach!

The Indian desert cat makes its home in the deserts of India, where temperatures can swing between a freezing 0°C in winter and a burning 50°C in summer.

Desert cats have evolved to thrive in the desert. They have hairy, densely padded paws, which allow them to walk on the blisteringly hot desert sand without burning their little feet.

One of the biggest challenges in a desert is finding water. These cats survive their dry environments by getting their water quota from their prey, just like leopards! They can go weeks without a sip of water.

Desert cat coats resemble desert sand with spots to mimic shadows and pebbles. The coat becomes lighter or darker depending on how hot their area is.

The desert cat's favourite prey includes desert jirds, gerbils and small birds. They are an adaptable species and are known to eat snakes, frogs and even the rare chicken from human habitations.

 DID YOU KNOW?

The desert cat is the closest relative of the house cat. The best way to tell them apart is to look at their ears and tails – desert cats have small tufts of hair pointing up from long ears and black-tipped tails with 2–5 black rings.

Desert cats are so rare and shy, we don't know exactly how many exist in India. But estimates suggest less than 500 individuals.

This is the only cat that lives in burrows like a fox!

Spot Them Here!

Follow the pug marks to find some of the best places to spot India's coolest cats!

Fact Finder

"Wild Cats: Status Survey and Conservation Action Plan". *IUCN*, 1995, https://portals.iucn.org/library/sites/library/files/documents/1995-062-En.pdf.

"Cat Territory Marking – All Cats Big and Small." *Conservation Cub Club*, https://conservationcubclub.com/cat-territory-marking-all-cats-big-and-small/.

"Bengal Tiger." *Encyclopædia Britannica*, https://www.britannica.com/animal/Bengal-tiger.

"Bengal Tiger." *National Geographic*, https://www.nationalgeographic.com/animals/mammals/facts/bengal-tiger.

"Asiatic Lion Behavior." *San Diego Zoo Library Guide*, https://ielc.libguides.com/sdzg/factsheets/lions/behavior.

"Snow Leopard." *Encyclopædia Britannica*, https://www.britannica.com/animal/snow-leopard.

"Snow Leopard Facts." *Snow Leopard Trust*, https://snowleopard.org/snow-leopard-facts/.

"Leopard." *Encyclopædia Britannica*, https://www.britannica.com/animal/leopard.

Weisberger, Mindy. "Clouded Leopard: The Cat with Saber-Like Teeth That Can Walk Upside Down in Trees." *Live Science*, https://www.livescience.com/animals/cats/clouded-leopard-the-cat-with-saber-like-teeth-that-can-walk-upside-down-in-trees.

"Prionailurus viverrinus." *Animal Diversity Web*, https://animaldiversity.org/accounts/Prionailurus_viverrinus/.

Sunquist, Mel, and Sunquist, Fiona. *Wild Cats of the World*. Chicago, University of Chicago Press, 2002.

"Caracal Crisis." *RoundGlass Sustain*, https://roundglasssustain.com/conservation/caracal-crisis.

Ghosh, Maitreya. "A Caracal Captured on a Camera Trap Renews Conservation Efforts." *Mongabay India*, https://india.mongabay.com/2025/04/a-caracal-captured-on-a-camera-trap-renews-conservation-efforts/.

"Caracal Facts." *Fact Animal*, https://factanimal.com/caracal/.

"Felis manul." *Animal Diversity Web*, https://animaldiversity.org/accounts/Felis_manul/.

"Pallas's Cat Facts." *Roundglass Sustain*, https://roundglasssustain.com/infographics/pallass-cat-facts.

"Himalayan Lynx: The Beautiful Cat of the Cold." *Greenverz*, https://greenverz.com/himalayan-lynx-the-beautiful-cat-of-the-cold/.

"All About Indian Desert Cat." *RoundGlass Sustain*, https://roundglasssustain.com/species/all-about-indian-desert-cat.

"Desert Cat – Cute Cat Living in the Desert." *Greenverz*, https://greenverz.com/desert-cat-cute-cat-living-in-the-desert/.

"Felis lybica." *IUCN Red List of Threatened Species*, https://www.iucnredlist.org/species/131299383/154907281

Credits

Writer: Yamini Srikanth

Designer: Anastasia Baliyan

Picture Credits

iStockphoto: Sourabh Bharti, #2177065565; Gannet77, #674191698; Dopeyden, #509182958; Photocech, #585082992; Thinker360, #1420676204; Sourabh Bharti, #1693429102; jbhavya, #537356122; SWAPNIL MEHTA, #1454113473; Karan Mota, #1297665246; aaprophoto, #1286762694; Miropa, #1219566867; Miropa, #1219566876; picture Umar, #2062965782; Martin Leber, #2178857566; guenterguni, #955522976; Banu R, #1407557845; Sourabh Bharti, #1492878037; pjmalsbury, #94973639; Sourabh Bharti, #1070688080; Sourabh Bharti, #1884972665; Banu R, #1441354008; Banu R, #1425117342; Sourabh Bharti, #1279091687; Robert Knofe, #1037573942; guenterguni, #1210401755; Miropa, #1219518963; Miropa, #1219518937; guenterguni, #1210401618; Rellerfl, #1453687914; wrangel, #481084422; Robert Knofe, #1037573922; maximilian-nils, #2205993269; guenterguni, #1210401698; tane-mahuta, #1292605624; Suman Biswas, #1195662392; Suman Biswas, #1195662505; AmitRane1975, #518110788; Rixipix, #1497364651; Sarah_Cheriton, #177434833; Koushik Bhattacharjee, #1266726638; Rufous52, #527882495; Michel VIARD, #1306654731; wrangel, #917624346; CampPhoto, #1092474326; Utopia_88, #629264484; davemhuntphotography, #156528526; wrangel, #623884592; wrangel, #615279814; slowmotiongli, #1226706821; KristinaPerlerius, #470096059; claudio.arnese, #1068261184; kamuil29, #531711852; StuPorts, #140071753; RichLindie, #1222025430; StuPorts, #166281634; Banu R, #1468246970; Marvin Samuel Tolentino Pineda, #1397299930; Banu R, #1468247006; maximilian-nils, #2205991817; cookelma, #2192263944; eli77, #487074633; Joppi, #1133170369; Andyworks, #672768678; slowmotiongli, #1254527684; SeppFriedhuber, #180736884; Luftaufnahme Bayern, #2157821565; svehlik, #172450736; svehlik, #490063401; Banu R, #1471410160; Rishi Kadikar, #1465954972; maximilian-nils, #2205993269; Sourabh Bharti, #2177065565.

iNaturalist: Asian Wildcat (Felis lybica ssp. ornata) by Raja bandi; Asian Wildcat (Felis lybica ssp. ornata) by Raja bandi; Asian Wildcat (Felis lybica ssp. ornata) by Raja bandi; Asian Wildcat (Felis lybica ssp. ornata) by Raja bandi; Asian Wildcat (Felis lybica ssp. ornata) by Mohammad Amin Ghaffari.

Pexels: Lynx Jumping After Stick During Training by Catherine Harding Wiltshire; cougar on Brown Grass by Frans van Heerden;

Unsplash: Brown lion lying on green grass during daytime by Vivek Doshi.

Wikimedia Commons: Bengal tiger by Tisha Mukherjee; Fishing Cat (Prionailurus viverrinus) by Cliff; Caracal (Caracal caracal) by Dirk Froebel; Manul (Otocolobus manul) in Zoo Zürich by Karin Sturzenegger; Lynx lynx isabellinus by Abujoy; Lynx lynx isabellinus by Abujoy; Lynx lynx isabellinus by Abujoy; Lynx lynx isabellinus by Abujoy; Asian Wildcat (Felis lybica ssp. ornata) by Лариса Артемьева; Lynx lynx isabellinus by Abujoy.

Independent sources: Pallas' Cat by Mohit Mehta; Desert Cat, DNP by Shashank Dalvi; Desert Cat by Dhyey Shah; Desert Cat by Dhyey Shah.

First published by Juggernaut Books 2025

Text copyright © Juggernaut Books 2025

10 9 8 7 6 5 4 3 2 1

P-ISBN: 9789353459581
E-ISBN: 9789353453763

All rights reserved. No part of this publication may be reproduced, transmitted, or stored in a retrieval system in any form or by any means without the written permission of the publisher.

Printed at Nutech Print Services - India